The Impossible

The Impossible

Poems by

Deborah DeNicola

Cover design by Shay Culligan

ISBN: 978-1-952326-96-7

Kelsay Books
502 South 1040 East, A-119
American Fork, Utah, 84003

For my sister, Deena Passler
1951-2018

Acknowledgments

Aesthetica: (U.K.) "Color Blind"
American Journal of Poetry: "He Drove Faster"
Ascent Aspirations: "The Abyss"
Briar Cliff Review: "Mother Incarnate" "Legacy"
Carpe Articulum: "The Tree at Tigertail" (published as "The Tree at Casa Cara" "Something Other"
Cadence "What She Was In For"
Common Ground: "Noah's Dove"
Heart: "Today" "Here for The Thanking" "Never My Birthday"
Lunarosity: "If Love Suffers Gladly"
Melusine: "Eve of my Evolution"
New Millennium: "Sun Song," "The Night as Meditation"
The New Verse News: "The Evening News"
Mid-American Review: "How To Face It"
Nimrod: "Aquarian Orpheus" (as "Reading Mark Strand") "Indulgences"
Oracle 20/20: "Feng Shui for Lovers" "Presence" (as "To Waken")
Packingtown Review: " Thirteen Ways of Looking at Hitchcock's Blackbirds"
Passager & The Passager Anthology: Burning Bright, "Let Love"
Poetry Pacific: "Yoga Stardust" "Tableau" "Transparent Man"
Salamander: "Being" "The Sorrow of the Body" "Deaths Dreams: After" "Deaths Dreams: The Clearing"
Solstice: "Rewind"
South Florida Poetry Journal: "Karma"
Prairie Schooner: "What Falls Away is Elsewhere"
Tiferet: "Without and Within"
Umbrella: "Reaching for my Prayer Book" "Perish the Thought"
Vox Populi: "What Words" "The Evening News"
Woven Tale Press: "The Impossible"

"Harmony of the Next" is the title poem from the award-winning chapbook from The Riverstone Poetry Chapbook Contest, Freedom, AZ.

Parts of "The World's Veil" first appeared in my memoir, *The Future That Brought Her Here,* published by Nicholas Hays/Ibis Press in 2009.

*

My sincere thanks to my comrades in poetry for the ongoing No Names Workshop and the National Endowment of the Arts for an individual artist's grant providing time for "The World's Veil."

Special thanks for blurbs from Leslie Ullman, most recently the author of *The You That All Along Has Housed You* and *Library of Small Happiness, Essays, Poems and Exercises on The Craft of Poetry.*

Kenneth Rosen, most recently the author of *Gomorrah,* and *The Origins of Tragedy.*

Lenny Dellarocca, founder and co-publisher of *The South Florida Poetry Journal.*

Grey Held, author of *Two Star General, Spilled Milk,* and *WorkaDay.*

Contents

III_ The World's Veil

IV The Evening News

Where was it one first heard of the truth?
The the.
—Wallace Stevens

I

The Big Enigma

Feng Shui for Lovers

Let the sun pour in from the east to drape your foyer.
Face the Matisse nude opposite the bed, and light the cherub
sconces on the mantle. Align the frangipani nebulizer
on the kitchen chopping block so it will waft into the bath.
Place the candles on the stairway and with each step your lover
will move farther into fire. Play Edith Piaf on the Ipod and leave
the Pinot Noir at room temp. String the ceiling with glow-
in-the-dark-stars. Slide onto the settee, wing one leg up, flip
an elbow out and point to the bedroom with a stationery toe.
Smoke the negligée over the bedpost, drop *Shakespeare's Sonnets*
on the nightstand. Leave some fallen petals across the marble
tiles. Half-mast the window so that the perfume
of your lilac tree will mist the glass.

Let Love

There is but one word—again.
—Miroslav Holub

In rooms of perfumed tapers, I've gluttoned on love.
Loved inside up and downside out. And loved again. Loved

the unavailable, the ambivalent . . . Have sworn
no more no more no more no more.

And the dreamy remtide of desire with its rudimentary swells,
its salve and ebb, its poxy crevices and desiccation—

that bottomless water-gazing, that grazing
mounting the dunes, the cresting run-off of the heart

has wracked this deciduous body so over and over,
so loving now through outbacked arteries just might be

the light-emitting-diode-version of myself.
Stablized. Simonized. Decelibatized

by letting go—*Let go—Let love!*
Without reciprocity. Without skittish kisses or

expensive mosts, or certificates of fantastic suffering.
Without apotropaic ovations, muttered stone-rubbing

spells, that enchantment and collapse,
(mea culpa, mea ultima culpa . . .)

Without withs and without withouts—
And God help us, without pre-s and posts, no

syntaxable legalese please—just the surge
of cheekbone and chi, glitter skin, gypsy hips,

glutes and tongue . . . flex and ascension
under sheeted fury. And whatever else,

and why not? When nothing comes close!
When we live to love, *love* to love—

so wherefore, therefore, why ever *not?*

The Lure

after Jane Hirshfield

A fleck of gold on the threshold
    of the heart's doorway

down the long corridor
    of the soul's true interest. We mix it

up with romance. We mix it up
    because we're mixed up, but our higher

selves are not. The lioness
    tastes the lure in her empty maw,

the goldness. She does not
    want to want, wants

to conquer want, wants to make
    matter from abstraction and

lap it up. But she knows only hunger,
    its waves slapping her tongue

as if gold could be spun
    from imagined taste. But the gold

is part—maybe all—(surely part)
    of the heart, as well—it is *why*

we walk in and out
    of this lure to stalk,

longing for gold
    we've already got—.

The Big Enigma

Le mystere contre nature. Bony abyss
bottomless stone, my own tomorrowing
torment. The antithesis of every painted paradise

down to the worst detail cf Dante, tears that turned
inward and froze into needles till the eyeballs bled.
It was the imagineless

imagined, sprinkled with untranslatables glyphs.
It flew off thought's runway in syllables
of flickering lightbulbs behind the dropped ceiling

of the mind's florescence, something scratching
under flocculence, a guttural growl through deceptive hemp.
The promise of morning flannel and fleece, skin's

most intimate admissions. Why deny it? That protean paradox
was always home in the thin periphery of your ear,
you heard it whisper, you swatted it back in summer

with a rolled magazine—even when it folded around your fingers
crossing the street, steering you beneath traffic and raining stars—
there by the marquee of the old Orson Welles,

down the cobblestone alley to the quaint graveyard
where you first met your love by a bouquet of chrysanthemums.
You were a thousand years young then, a mantilla of faith

of your shoulders and too soon left, a museum piece, decorative
prayer on a shelf of the Self's mausoleum. It lay down inside you.
Before you noticed, it took. And took everything.

And threw the key away.

He Drove Faster

Much faster than he could think.
He drove as if his I.Q. was one hundred and eighty.
He drove like a gangster with twenty-one carat lug nuts,
like a bandit stashing his sock of slugs in the glove
compartment. He drove with one hand on the wheel
at two o'clock, one arm out the window, palm
on the side-view mirror he never checked.
He drove like Monty, like Jimmy Dean, like Bond
in his Aston Martin or Cary Grant in *North by Northwest*—
And she sat shotgun without a seatbelt—not
mandated yet—She sat composed like Grace Kelly,
like Eva Marie Saint looking down at the yawning canyons,
felt herself like the road, foreign and flat.
Fuel-ingesting, never-ending.

The Light in Aix

Were all Flowers once wild? Of course. Like I was wild
in my strip-poker phase at fourteen, devoted to playing
Hearts and *Knuckles* with Jimmy K. behind the snack bar,
beach roses heaving like nubile breasts along the clam flats.
Later, eighteen, tanned and untamed, a bit more seedy
like the sunflowers in southern France among
lavender and cypresses where the sun never set
on the back of Guillaume's bike. Then hitching alone,
just me and the light in Aix. At twenty-five, sweet
gardenia I tried to cultivate, coax into blossom,
newly married, already wilting in northern kitchens.
Norwegian stove kindled with cedar, the rooms for living,
cold. Some flowers fail in domesticity, some canker to rust.
So I hurled myself hard—into the future—which absolves
the past after all, once and for all.

Karma

You were the smuggler of just-let-me-get-by.
I was your fence in the outside world, star
that burnt out but left you a light

to smother in quilts of denial. I was the one
who disturbed double-entendres
with my euphemisms and underlit puns.

I was the whisper insisting we down that laced drink,
transit to a zip code beyond belief in the construct of time.
I was the synapse bridging neurons of untransmuted desires.

You were the ear-worm of *Cm'ere/Go away,*
Cm'ere/Go away—while I went undercover, snooping
through classified documents, false flags, big lies

under recycled debris. I was the believer
in spite of contrary evidence, the quiver
to raise your genetic vibration, gateway

to golden-age orgasm. I was the booty call
you overlooked, mistook for a dim alley
when I actually led into truth town. You—

of the bad accent, brutal biceps and occasional slur,
you—the broken river's poison. You were the dumpster
I dropped into, packaged wreckage, damned spot

I dared rub hard with Clorox and dollar-store products.
You—the Houdini whose costume malfunctioned, that slip
into underworlds I'd risen out of. You were *that guy,*

nailed to exigencies of the past. I was
'la crème de la crème' coffee houses couldn't
surpass, so rich and sweet no one could swallow—

Together our souls were unbalanced masses on Zeus's scales,
taxed by the rumors of colleagues, separated
by highway truck stops and side effects

of prescription drugs. Despite these
minor differences, I loved you then,
I love you now—.

The Abyss

It's the way oblivion carries you in its quilted sarcophagus.
No use for a rung underfoot or a roof overhead. One night
you were loved, the next night you forgot how to read,
found only soap operas on television. I've learned

to seek non-being. Luge into the boggy void, yank up a frog
by its raggedy leg and kiss it. Though it's difficult to sit in,
the abyss is a sacred state. Your mind no longer bloated
with ribboned gifts, weepy apologetics, divine recipes

for butterfish. You have to fight to keep it empty—
Lay out its light behind clouded glass. At least
you can always name nothingness: *Dishpan Dun,*
Indigo Neon, Gun-metal Chevrolet—

or that shade of lipstick you wore in grad school,
Wine With Everything.

Transparent Man

He taught himself how to make colors transparent.
Make the roof of the sky and its blue go away.
Birds taught him how to braid words encrypted as nests.

And I learned how to survive in the forest with only
a tarp and plastic utensils. He taught me bad magic,
his tall fingers tendrilled my throat, and I choked out
the very big questions he'd later knot in my hair.

Only the fires could trace him, each like a Siamese sign
or a semaphore, embers astray in translation, smoky
remnant of notes we had sung. And the villagers swore
he could square circles through different dimensions.

Sometimes even now when night sifts through my hair,
I shrink into shadow, feel for him there with my tongue.

Never My Birthday

I don the hairshirt of the heart commanding Creator to deliver
my ex-lover once again. And I am patient, divine timing, *snowy
egret of regret*—all that. But one day—weather for open
sunroofs—weather of wanting, wind warm but not oppressive,
I see him perfectly parallel park his Lexus in front of La Tratorria

Café. I stand by the umbrella tables—*poached salmon—blue
cheese butter*—Oh *mimosa of the heart*—To see him stride toward
me after so many years, his ring finger finally bare and touching
the thumb like a Buddhist mudra. *Namaste,* I whisper through the
smoking robe of my heart. The past is a leopard inside me.

But it's never my birthday, always his fireworks. *Oh whiplash—
Oh Magpie—Oh unregistered gun of the heart*—variants
of a hostile future. Dear Lord, he is my walking electrocution.
The jolt of his presence slightly more than an aftershock shimmy
under the sidewalk. Epidermis in a furnace, I am vaporized by old

lies shot into the brokered mattress of our love life—*Rock opera
of the heart—Mosh pit of the heart*—In my mind-waters, fish burnt
to soot, algae choking on nightshade and hemlock—I step into
the hedge denying him entrance—*Black armband* of the heart,
Chapter Eleven of the decomposed, composted heart.

Legacy

Tommy Huck had a box of matches and knew how to light them.
His brother, Billy, said they'd practiced at home in the bathroom
and now Tommy was a pro—. At the edge of the desert path
the tumble weeds rolled like witches' heads, and I imagined
coyotes I'd heard howl at night with their savage heads thrown
back. That eerie sound, an orange napalm cloud. So I guess

I wasn't surprised at the spread of the flames, brighter than sun
on the dry grass that broke into a circus of fire as the wind
sparked the bank's furry mane leading down to the river,
where wild weeds broke into colors of autumn—October,
the sun already swung low in the afternoon, and my six-year-old
body shook with the thrill as the twin brothers ran away.

I loved them but didn't love their leaving me with incinerating
water, alone—to find the path back to the land where I would be
safe. Soon sirens came, and my mother appeared running toward
me—Once home she sent me to my room where I sat with my
Golden Books, looking for lions, recalling the gold jaws of the fire

and how time speeded up, how my mother was angry the two boys
coerced me into their trap. Right there, right then, with those
badass twins—my love of danger was born—How this memory
pushed me—how far I would go to get close to the burning—
that dictated, twenty years later, what kind of men I would love.

Christmas Morning

I wait for my son to pick me up at the Air B.N.B.
while an icy winter fastens to early light
sifting through stripped and stranded trees,

the ground, not exactly strafed—though it couldn't
raise a twig as windchill freezes silence-tight.
Oh, but the light is fine from behind the window

where I stand imagining if the quiet could speak
what it might say to these evergreens, the only fertile
color among mountains of driftwood and weeds.

We are not far inland on this small island where
I come to visit every Christmas. But beyond the pane
there are no wreaths, no tinsel, no tourmaline-

lake lit up like the one I saw in Galilee—though a stable
might be nestled deep in these woods—behind that singular
lamp-post that insists this is not the wilderness

where Jesus wandered, not the 40-day-desert-thing
and no Luciferian temptation offers me power and a city.
I think I might get lost, fall down the stony road—

Though—this no man's land, this stillness,
might offer enlightenment . . . So I wait in this stranger's
drafty home to which my son is late. Then a blast

from the furnace—and origami birds twirl from the ceiling,
but still no cars grace the barren road, not my son's Infiniti,
not even a horse and buggy, no camels or donkeys trotting by—

Nonetheless, it's a sacred scene because of the sunlight
slipping in and out of the naked thicket like some message
written in ancient Aramaic among shadows that elongate,

as if they could stretch my remaining faith and cure me
of all my thinking, all my wanting while I wait in this world
for all ages and all aging to finally be done. I stand

by the window, like a figure in a Hopper painting,
as if a redeemer is really deep in this mythic woods,
a savior nailed and bleeding from palms and feet, held

by mothering trees, consoling despite the suffering.
As if he truly was born to bear the sins of our monstrous world—
and beyond that—born today, born specifically for me.

Tonight I Have Fallen

into Neruda's forgetting—remembering now, how
"forgetting is so long—" Remembering how much
I've forgotten of loving and I love remembering

which lets loose a swarm of lovers, the ones never dreamt
away, tossing in reverie's brevity, forgivenesses all dancing
under kind stars or cruel starless nights—under wine stains,

under threadbare sheets, light lapping through bedroom
windows, rooms superimposed—videos of forgotten faces
as the body glows—electric—*No,* Whitman would not say

love is brief. Love Whitmanesque suspends—hot
as a song can torch, crooned into memory's heat, while
his love draws out the heart's venom so it may be pure

once more and roar. Lion heart looming over the doorsill.
And Bukowski said *Love is a dog from hell.* Indeed,
and need is a wild darling. Sometimes darkness wants

to hike out of the heart's gullies, brush off the bugs
and burying sand, while lightning flies in crystal thistles.
Love opens its mouth like that dog from hell,

deep throat of gusto—its tongue so adept at both rapture
and torment—Such ardor, so whole, such love is *Jesus-
Come-to-Momma,* newborn cherub testing its wingspan,

lifting gravestones, riding particles of the hearts let loose
from the bodies that lie there open-hearted with longing
in their middle names—Longing in rags, traipsing

from village to village, splayed crutches out front, blind sins
like stray cats limping behind, sins trapped in the potholes
of broken roads. And how longing lies about being alone

when solitude is—as well—a loving companion
that makes room for memory, flashes forward
then back to what still lives in recall, fantasy

motored by nothing but breathing, breathing
by only acceptance, accepting forgiveness,
forgiving with will.

The Tree at Tigertail

Just off Route One
before Tigertail Corner, there's a gargantuan banyan
with limbs like Gothic buttresses.

I step in, genuflect, walk the labyrinth of shadow,
and I am once again at Chartres.

No cars come by. The bells of birdsong cease
and all is pagan subtext. I am at worship, welling
at the root with the woivre underground. Leaves

of blue shoulder the spires, light sculpts itself into gates
as if the Madonna deep in the crypt, in sync with me,

rejuvenates. And I don't know if I have penance or license
here in Miami's medieval groves where centuries
flow and coalesce. Early in adolescence, safe

behind the hedge of our suburb's borders,
I wandered with him to find a place to lie

and kiss. There was no canopy like this
but we erected pleasure
in the hammock of a willow. I would have sworn

vows to the tree's virgin goddesses, but for the body's
coveting touch, soft branching skirts that rush

and juncture, here and here . . . though I have as much
these years after lust—summoning rapture
below and above. It took generations

and scaffolds and fires, great wheels, Black
Madonnas and Templar monks—*lifetimes*
to raise that cathedral to its finish. And while

clouds burn off, the tree at Tigertail
reaches morphogenetic hallways while
the tablet of my hand glows, alchemical,

cobalt to emerald. His name was Jim—
We were so very young, domed
beneath the natural burgeoning,

past the pillars into the nave.

The Night as Meditation

—After Wallace Stevens

In the dark eco-
  system of sleep, psyche
unfolds
  and floats
above the moment
  that matters
    most, the one that oils
imagination
  where dreaming
begins. Penelope alone
  in her husband-hewn

bed. Or asleep at the loom,
  threads fallen
to water
  where his jury-rigged raft
    is eaten
  by carnivorous algae.

And the sun—
  a rise of harp strings
ghosting the ocean.
  Penelope's shuttle rushes
like a comber
  that tousles grains of sand
in synch. Or the breeze

  sweeping the air
whisking it thither in lush
  exhalations.

That lavish force
        not dissimilar
to desire. Penelope's
        sighs

loosen cascades
        of twine
        to climb the
mythic fount
        of him again. To create
is
to become. Odysseus

lives
    within the tapestry as she weaves
him on and on,
                    sustains the seas'
buoying
        arms
despite the Gods'
        ordinances.

Here—
        her will is for
sensing
        how
        to sew herself
in.

The Impossible

They could not understand why he had a wife and she a husband.
—Chekov, "The Lady with the Dog"

Rain today. Sepia tinting the onion domes in St. Petersburg square,
and they can scarcely remember Yalta that August when the lilac-
hued water sparked the harbor and current surged between
them like lit kerosene. Perhaps if she hadn't walked her white
Pomeranian down to the sea. Perhaps if it had bitten Dmitri
or peed on his summer shoes—and Anna—so taken with his hair—
how it tinseled in sunlight. By nightfall she'd fallen through

his sturgeon-blue eyes. Even after they parted, abandoned their
sultry moon neither realized the damage done in that hotel room,
though Anna wore her guilt like the heavy crimson drapes. And as
each returned to the proper—*(but so mediocre)*—spouse, something
within Dimitri shifted, broke open—this late in his life, to peer
through a lorgnette and see up close a new world within—
the self from a foreign realm, forgotten but true, a self

soft as goose down, one who found joy in daily life—but
"How? How?" Dimitri cried. And why *now,* between these rough
kisses, after his tower of dalliances amounted to nothing?
After he'd settled for brief salvos of cheating year after year,
all kept from his intimidating wife. Why had this fading angel
lanced his heart so that dread bled when he—who had always
been immune—found love now as a lethal injection

envenoming the future. And Anna, months later, that night in S—
annoyed by even the thought of her flunky husband, looked up
from her muff as she met Dimitri on the back stair of the opera
house, his formal coat, his silk cravat—her fair hair falling in
weepy locks—when they couldn't help but swallow the space
spinning between their bodies—couldn't help but inhale those
wafting intoxicants down the long road ahead to the impossible.

II

Indulgences

Mother Incarnate

My mother asleep on the chaise with the moving water adjacent.
We two, only residents at the pool, late spring afternoon,
long shadows from the high-rise swaddle the lounges.
Dark towels of treetops fold over brick tiles. Supple sun
in the rails of the catwalk. Slatted shadow cast on the grounds.

Always the dark and the light, dark and light. The pooled water
keeps moving because the wind is up and the palms are passing
it between them finger by finger, a rush of messages
only a mystagogue might decipher. The swish and wash
of the breeze complements the clouds rumpling

toward comfort. The water goes where the wind says and the
voices of gulls follow. The water moves because the wind says
something moving, what a mother might say to her daughter
calming her worries before she must sing for a crowd. I remember
my mother praying always, now almost cheerfully waiting to die,

breath expectant each night. Like anyone, she'd prefer to pass
over in sleep. Proud mother who says out loud nonetheless,
she's aware of her mind's decay, under crimped skin, aware
of a silkworm lighting her limbs, something spoken in code
by trees and shadows. Small strokes like those that skirt across

water. One spark burnt here, one brain cell's invisible damage,
memory's chemicals draining away. The skull visible
behind her smile. What life did. What it does to us all.
The truth of my mother incarnate at ninety in the sun-downing
hour, my own head deflowering like hers. In this moment

we're two peonies weighted with sun. How they sing
in our living faces, afloat, dozing upright.

After The Stroke

Often she speaks of a mysterious *They*. "When are *They* coming?"
"Where are *They?*" "Do *They* all do that, wear that, eat that?"

"Must we pay *Them?*" But she forgets everything in a matter
of minutes: rooms, news, rules of a favorite card game.

And she forgets she forgets. Objects, once familiar, disappear,
surface again in surprising places: Scotch tape in the medicine

cabinet, jewelry under the sink, cash in the refrigerator drawer.
Still she wants to help me in the kitchen. Sets the table with folded

wax paper and sheets of foil for napkins. And she sneaks chocolate
pudding for breakfast. Watches cartoons or the Spanish soaps.

Her eyes grow small and dim in a thinning face. Her hair,
which she always wore in a neat French knot, is loose and sparse

down her shoulders, although, vanity remains intact. She applies
mascara to her eyebrows, powders wrinkles flat, blushes her nose,

loops a scarf through a buttonhole, clutches an evening bag to her
bath robe. Old friends no longer call. Her daughters have her

sisters' names. Each night she strings different words in a chain
and repeats them a hundred and fifty times. Sometimes there's

a question she means to ask but she can't find a sentence,
sputters sparks instead. She wants to go home when she is home.

And when angry with me, my mother hisses . . .
I hope you live this long.

Indulgences

There's no breeze in this heat, just one leaf
in this bush shaking slowly. And when my hunger
enters the sky that holds me, it knows no bounds,
encompasses consciousness I can shade
like O'Keefe's numinous mounds—
and I remember my favorite saints, Theresa and Joan,
how they offered their suffering up as the nuns
instructed us—but I offer nothing to no one today,
passing the Sorenson gallery in downtown Delray.
How odd these huge flowers hang in the windows

just when I'm thinking of her desert skulls
and how bones are said to contain the soul
of the animal, which is why saints have reliquaries
and one must pay Rome for a toenail that bestows
an "Indulgence" for sin. I wonder why the old clergy
called them "Indulgences" when they were meant
to wipe out negative stains, meant most as release from evil.
I imagine pastel emanations like orbs skating over my skin,
little ionizations that sanctify the horse heads in Georgia's
canvases—like Magritte's tuba amid that blue sky.

Georgia made more of the natural landscape
than I find in these Caribbean boutiques. And Magritte
certainly knew how two disparate items juxtaposed
produce something surreal between them. Maybe I'm just
tincturing the avenue with my sky-high blues, bequeathed
from my long-gone father. I think of him rather than
Mother whose dementia hangs over her wheelchair
like a stain in her bluish halo though she won't qualify
for canonization. I picture the mantle of "caretaker"

my friends project onto me, when it's really tristesse
that a life comes to this—not quite cerulean solid
like the pillowy cloud O'Keefe painted behind one horse
which itself is combed with pinks and yellows, pale
in the long teeth, pleats like liquefied caves in the shape
of mandorlas. And every state in my mind's mansion
is an entrance into blue, even the punctured holes
in the bird's eye view of the skull as if someone nailed it
to the horizon. And if I were holy, I just might drop
through my mother's stigmata and come out cleansed.

One New Year's Eve years ago the two of us killed
a whole bottle of Amaretto and I badgered her
to reveal the truth behind my father's early death.
She'd lived the lie so long she believed it, and I was
in therapy, once again enraged at a man. I was ruthless.
Now I'm older, remorseful for the atrophy
of her thinning body, wishing she'd sprout wings
and fly away. On my bureau there's a photo of us
that Christmas under the tree—tinseled together
on my flowered sofa. Her face is soft and round

and feminine, deep as an O'Keefe lily, prominent
cheekbones like back in the day—My smile's nailed
across my face, our skulls so close together,
how can I not see my own fate, how can I not look away?
Wrapped in Florida's firmament, no matter how
gem-like its azure, I see O'Keefe's string-like strokes,
the cartilage of that horse, scaffolding in the sky
and my mother's skeletal shadow. Her husband by his own
hand done in, and me with my bad taste in men, ready
to face the desert canvas again, begin my next life.

How To Face It

I empty my whisper into her ear each night with the 23rd psalm,
lower my voice into that cradle of death, pretend
she remembers we traveled there together years ago, though

in truth, she remembers nothing—Not Israel, the moon-cratered
landscape, the black caves and lavender limestone. Nor carnage
at Masada, the outline of Herod's troops, a sickle in sand.

Not the treacherous Roman road under the hairpin turns
of the tour bus or how I put rocks in my pockets to take back
to my Jewish friends. Here in the hospital bed she's safe, she's

home. At least the wallpaper here is a kind of green pasture.
Here she floats above the still waters. But she can't roll over
on her own, can't walk or eat or pee alone. She can't speak.

Who could believe—her eyes glazed in film since the stroke—
that her brain flashes with recognition as I slip my fingers
through her slim, boneless grip? I smile and squeeze, zoom

in to tug at her smile, which happens. The sweet, upturning
vine of her mouth happens on its own. She knows it's bath
and bedtime. She's alert, a reptilian bird, sculpted bones

of her face under crepe-thin skin. I recall years of watching her
dress, adding water droplets to a cake of mascara then stroking
in layered tiers, then her lipstick-brush lining and filling.

I realize I love her most here at the end as I love my own life
for the first time really, because she shows me how to trek
the shadowed valley, how to live when you're almost dead.

Today

Today I live with my elderly mother in a condominium on a finger canal in Florida. She's demented from a major stroke and a couple of hundred T.I.A.'s. I am now an unemployed Adjunct Professor from Boston who finds Florida surreal, the invisible pool with its glinting surface, edgeless edges, surreal. The view from the porch to the tied boats, surreal. In the distance, sails and malls and malls and malls, another canal, another lanai, another invisible pool, surreal.

I've hired two angels from Jamaica. They speak English in another language, softer vowels, swifter strings of sounds that knit a net to catch my mother and me when we fall. And we all fall while the skies dance. Cloud formations amass above our heads and down our halls. The sun has many colors, many moods. The air, imperious, water, ubiquitous. I am not in control though I have legal documents, the D.N.R. on the refrigerator so the E.M.T.'s will know. We've had it with hospitals, although my mother may live forever mindless.

I am connected by cells, by webs of sea weed, coral junctures. I dance three times a week in a mirrored studio with other women, come home, swim in the surreal pool, cook dinner, usually fish. I have no path, no plan. Like my mother, I am living in the *Now*. My mother is dying of course, as are we all. Today, however, no one here is dead. I sit by the rails of the porch amazed how the palms tremble though they're grounded into earth. I watch the mother duck out-waddle her babies after dunking them in the drink. I am buffered by bougainvillea, periwinkle leaves, bruise-colored clouds. Hot pink and yellow frangipani, fragrant as a funeral home.

A green iguana visits. Though my mother has no mind she has no pain. I think this is because she's lost her thinking. Though I see the unity I'm part of, like my mother, I am no one. My own mind jumps like an orangutan after this thing called fulfillment.—Only my heart replies, *Maybe you have fulfillment when you are nobody.*

Mother Update

for My Brothers

She knows who I am. Even knows when I wonder
if she knows, and she needn't remember what she is,
another living being—existence's not worth pondering
when she's lost face and space, the date, the night—
though she still surrenders to the drapes that open
every day when what we used to call the light comes in.

She may not recognize the color blue but she knows
there's a soothing something out there when we're
wheeling by the sea. She wouldn't spell it right or
know what color is, but the ambiance of rooms
and walls do make a difference. She's accepted how
her mind flickers as if a silent movie. But no anger any
longer, having finally traded words for breath.

Yesterday could be tomorrow or Monday's Tuesday
and objects have no names. She doesn't tamper
with the motors of her body, their switches having faded
into other arms that lift and sit her like the dolls
she gave me in that other dream time. All is smaller
and more quiet, but she appreciates the jacarandas,
watches as I water and place them on the table.

She's often busy folding edges of tablecloths and blouses,
pleats and wraps a cookie in a napkin for the gift it is.
Her eyes say thank you—though her voice cannot—
—for the sparkly slippers comforting her feet. Those feet
have lost their function, and the word itself won't mean
a thing. But she gets a gesture's tenderness
though neither of us can imagine there's a word for it.

What She Was In For

While he stumbled through freezing cornfields and tented
tobacco patches. While he grew blind from frozen stars
on his eyelashes and tugged at the nubby wool of his coat

like some frostbitten Zhivago. Seeing only her face, a vision inside
the white landscape, her chestnut eyes, her cheekbones like snow
dunes, the upturned drift of her nose. Home, by the wood stove

in her parents' farmhouse, she filed her nails and read
the Sunday funnies. While he counted on a stranger's directions
from the train, she quietly gloated over her walk-out, how she'd

grabbed her bag, spun on her heels and hailed a cab to the station.
It was not that my mother did not love my father. After all,
he was a doctor and handsome as Cary Grant.

She just lacked compassion for passion, behavior she called
nonsense or neurosis. Like the time he turned on a sprinkler inside
her apartment. Not her idea of a joke. And how about the Picasso-

kitchen-painting-caper, or the samba on the table, drinking warm
beer from her nursing shoe? So when she saw him out the frosted
window, despite her delight, she stonewalled, stomped upstairs

to her old bedroom, adjusting the combs in her upswept chignon,
taking her time applying mascara, lipstick and blush,
till her wizened mother in her dotted babushka, huffed up the stairs

to tell her daughter this fair-haired Italian boy from Brooklyn,
this skinny intern whom her brothers, Mitchell, Henry and Joseph,
were feeding kielbasa, perogies, and vodka, this heartsick Romeo,

was suddenly jovial, entertaining them all—
Shouldn't she have known, if she married him,
what she was in for?

The Goose Girl's Foot

The Lladro Goose Girl lay on the coffee table
in Mother's living room for years. For years
she watched the clear martinis drain. She wasn't sad

to be broken. She didn't mind time, didn't mind change—
just stared at the flower in her hand, its eternal blooming.
And mother adored her. Years later, deep in dementia,

Mother tried to glue the foot back on with cold cream.
That was before she stopped talking, that was when
she could still walk, when she surprised us daily,

soup poured into a wine glass . . . Soon enough,
she lived in the fog of a body almost brainless.
To lose a foot—to lose a mind! What creatures are we

that parts of us break off? At the end she shut her eyes
for a week, shut lips, refused to eat. In the last hours
her eyes flew open, fixed on a point I couldn't contact,

and a slight cry leaked from her silence,
while the *Lacrima Mortis* swelled down one cheek.
I could see what work it was for her to die at ninety-five,

even with Hospice nearby and morphine under the tongue.
For hours, her skin incrementally purpled, the way her brain
blackened as the million thieves swept in. While my mother

labored into death I wrung her mottled hands, hoping
each breath would be the last. *Oh my mother, my rock,
so whole, so gorgeous*—gone to a ghost before my eyes.

Good neighbor, John, glued the Goose Girl's foot back on
the week after Mother died. Where I had failed,
my fingers stuck, he focused deftly—made that foot fit.

The Day After Your Death

Just me and my tears with the ninety-five years
of your body. Just me and the white roses I sent.
You wore the pink caftan you'd picked out twenty years
prior with your brain still intact. And I spoke to you
dead, the same way I had through the years of dementia.

Eventually you'd give a cold stare for conversation,
but you were still in your body, someone strange and new,
but still you. Alone in the undertakers' room
I knelt on the leather bar, apologized for the cremation.

I knew you wanted your body flown up north unimpaired.
As the years trudged by I'd seen the vacancy sign
in your eyes, became parent to your child and there
in the green funeral parlor, the room fragrant and full
with my white roses, no one else but us two

till I felt you, bodiless beside me in the coruscating air.
I knew it was you because my heart was on fire.
Your flesh, un-embalmed, smooth and blushed,
ready to burn. Then there were two of us bent
like the roses over the tinder, the ripening husk.

Yoga Stardust

Does light serve as breath? How do the meshed
colors of sky move inside to pump plumes
through my lungs? My vinyasas

on porcelain tile. A small chill tightens
my hands, and I want The Higher Nothingness,
the *Nothing* in perfect balance with the fans

rasping across from each other. Around me,
the patio doors are open, dust of stars I am
composed of, I go golden under this blue moon

gloaming like the stars dunked in the canal.
I am my atoms' patterned gleam, the poinciana's scarlet,
each molecule in that pile of muscle shells.

I am fallen palm next to drying towel.
A lizard skitters down the stucco wall, crosses
my plasma-painted toe, thinks it a hot rock to lie on.

But I rise to warrior, gently wobble him off.
Small pearl of peace, curled like his tail,
chi in my upturned palm.

Where She Is Now

The earth's poles are shifting and my mother has fallen
off of this world. She is no place I can see through.
I look inside her moonstone ring at the softening hues

of heaven, not colors I believe in really—though I visualize
butterflies on a butter-colored day, clover and ladybugs,
her azaleas and touch-me-nots—I imagine her standing

in the driveway of our old suburban home, leaning
on the car door as she hoses down the fieldstone path.
Summer. A temperate climate mixed with her Shalimar

musk. Sounds of cicadas or ribbiting peepers announcing
the new season where she is now. I see through memory's
embraces—that she's just gone inside the house.

For the umpteenth time, she's straightening the toy closet.
The game boards, the tokens, all the dolls on one shelf.
The puzzle pieces back in their places.

Tableau

On my mother's patio above the canal
I noticed a marriage in the clouds. Not only
loose doves, but small animals feeding

each other like Adam's hand clasped
to the Lord's in the Sistine sky. I watched
from the terrace. I saw the man-cloud

and the woman up high surrender
and touch, an angel buoyed between them
like the reverend who witnesses

the vows. I was witness. I saw Jerusalem
palms loft into firmament, creation's
first foreground. Then an aisle

of pageantry down which the clouds
stepped and met, one towards the other.
Male and Female He made them

in the rose tinted carpet of twilight
while completely oblivious,
the rock 'n' roll boats putted by.

III

The World's Veil

A Sequence about My Father's Death and Imagined Afterlife

*. . . and I will give a white stone, and on the stone is written
a new name that no one knows except the one who receives it.*
— Revelation 2:17

i. The Sorrow of the Body

Always at the edge of morning, when the curves
of the moon have faded, he expected clarity,
the exact latitude where color smudged the sky.
From where had the thought of paradise descended?

Behind the water tower, the dirt cliffs hung
over the polluted bay. Their depressions
matched his own and he was drawn to drive
beneath them while the city's beaten horizon

suggested this human tie to time was wrong.
Why did his dreams persuade him of huge, bottomless
stairways inverting the proper proportions of space
and rain? And what did it mean

when he woke in a trough of sighing, unaware
of any image for his ache? What held him aloft
were pastel reaches across the geographies,

to imagine them within grasp, as if they were facts,
or as if he could lance the body's gravity, withstand its tug
when the colors of the quarry rocks embraced each other,
when the sky at evening drained its pink

and green and gold into the small receptacle of a planet
whose belief in its own isolation sets a world to yearning—

Sweet yearning for the beauty of touching with the heart
what the mind did not—in creating the sorrow of the body.

ii. Being

He thought he could cut the cord to his regrets
by curing the world of its wounded.

He didn't know what he railed against
was its unfit heart. The lie it had sworn by—
this wormy marriage of life to death. He wanted

to dissect the body's burden, explore its incarcerated
god, *Spirit* draped in the body's grace. To wrap sun
beneath skin like a beacon and pivot each muscle,

distilling a glow deep in the veins. He thanked the body
for its blood, delicate cartilage like squid, wedged
appendages, nodes of marrow . . .

Dispensing medicine to carry the body's cargo
would not delay aging, but like anyone,
he wanted to prolong the music of youth.

Playing the staff of his wife's neck
as she sat in the freshly cut grass
lifting an infant to her shoulder.

He'd have willingly taken the toddler's steps
from beach to ocean, believing the waves' illusion
of movement, his feet wedged in damp sand,

not knowing earth's borders from water's,
not knowing his own, knowing nothing at all—
being.

iii. What Held Him Aloft

for so long was how whole he somehow
knew he was. Not how his mind saw it,
the fractured past tethered in place.
But he was amazed that he had made, after all,

children. Amazed at the body's responses
to love. How he honored the systems, the networks
of veins, the vapors and tremors of passion—

To lift his scalpel, to stitch the torn sinew of people
with families and names, to deliver them back—this
was a reason, *an answer*—enough to keep him in balance,

enough to replenish his well of faith. He'd look at his
own hands in wonder, envision the satiny heat
of healing, his own Hippocratic certificate,

an entitlement worth a life.

iv. To Rule the World

Under his dominion then,
an intravenous needle would deepen
the light in the crevice
between membrane and mucous.

One touch of his speculum and Spirit would open
inside, where he could probe a vibration
into song. He knew this was all anyone wanted—

to make music from misery, to hold the notes
of compassion for invasions of pain.

What the world did to the body was shameful
but he understood through connective tissue,
the vascular system's muted blues

so close to the skin,
the intricate hints at the body's veil—

Yet he misunderstood the mind's power, its
paranoia, didn't know why—
when he slid intuition down the crack
of the mind, he was confused
by the distance back.

To live inside loss was to believe
you were nothing
more than human, to rule the world out

of your life, until you were nothing
but cavity, matter, lacking Spirit's
eternal ember, which is light, *life*—
the soul in the body's world.

v. Lost in the Call

The yacht club docks shimmered whiter
      against those glazed summer nights,
wives in spaghetti straps with champagne glasses
      fluted to match their shapely heels,
fumes of dusky *Taboo* and musky
         Chanel in the air.

While Como and Crosby crooned
      their hi-fi foxtrot and money chimed
through the lair of paper lanterns,
      the effervescent surgeon carried
         a habit in his pocket.

Though for a time he could sing, samba,
      even fandango with the sucking monkey
on his back, the pills added up, multiplying
      the swarm of moons pulling him under
      the malted bay.

And there in his head both sibyls and sirens
warned and lured. *What path to travel?*
      Who could he call?
      Where was the cure?

vi. Can the Soul Be Insulted?

He dreamt of a rosebud broken through the sidewalk
in front of his old Brooklyn home. Something doomed
he wanted to water, force-bloom to a hothouse aura,

one small miracle in Caesar's world. He dreamt of tumbling
a wad of cash from his wallet, a confusion of Wall Street
and the Aqueduct Race Track, Lord & Taylor's, Sear's or

Sacks—an endless list of modern comforts: tvs, convertibles,
cruises. If his soul was insulted, it must have turned
the other cheek, its resistance less than the rose—

beaked wren whose tail he chased nightly, tossing salt.
He dreamt he was starving at a banquet, trampled
by maestros in tuxes and wingtips, contessas

in sequins and fur, saw himself crawling past loud
greedy guards excessively fed—his flesh
gone to famine, his soul left for dead.

vii. The Day of His Passing

he drove his two older children to the high school went home and
painted with dissatisfaction then followed his wife around the house
as she did her chores when she said she was going for groceries he
panicked begged to go with her without confessing his concerns
unaware he was desperate she left him abandoned addicted to the
secret of which she'd had but myopic glimpses he then went to the
medicine cabinet wrote himself another prescription maybe he
forgot how many pills were a limit forgot the toll morphine in
Demerol takes—but maybe he knew *yes somewhere he knew* and
when his daughter called after school wanting a frock for the prom
she'd been asked to he only seemed slightly distracted offered his
charge cards before he left in his snazzy sports car for the pick-up
where he ordered a slice of pie at the drugstore coffeeshop a drive
from which he did not come back since his body stopped when his
lungs collapsed.

viii. Deaths Dreams: In the Beginning

after the crash of the astral firmament,
after the end of his three-dimensional world,
above the fog of fragments and etheric arrivals,

the old geometries dissolved, recombined
into new alignment. And ruin departed
dragging its bag of grief. His breath quickened,

an intimacy redeeming the air—And he sensed
the ancient tinctures there as if he were witness
to the birth of extinct plants. Apparitions appeared

in the rivers over which hung trees blossoming
stars whose light shone like evening windows
in his memory's home. Each awakening,

an invisible impulse, entered his body's
sleeve of chakras, those wells of magnetic
photons snaking the temple empty

of bones—where filaments glowed
in a pillar of light, their source,
inexplicably known.

ix. Deaths Dreams: The Clearing

He was so far up in the mountains,
layers of blue haze, the tops of trees,
pine, fir, birch and beech—as if seen

from a plane. A thousand arms held up,
palms open, bent at the wrist and quiet snow
poised in the air like dusk. a grainy otherness,

when someone said they were serving heron,
and he saw Heron! *Blue,* with the head on,
the eye still as it lay on its side, restless

like a fish (though he thought to himself—*bird)*
as if he'd been swollen with heron
and all reminiscences, nostalgias

released from the breast—as if he had *lived*
in the fish-eyed bird, knew what the body felt
paralysed on the platter. And he knew

he would partake in the libations,
drink from the decanter—
If he bowed his head in clear intention,

this tie-dyed belt of light
would cinch in the clouds—
all heron on earth would wing to a clearing,

fish would leap to the higher frequencies
of their waters, while the snows resumed
their white contritions.

x. After

the first beautiful blitz of death, rain
and a tenderness he forgave
in every breathing thing.
Hyacinths. Marshes. Garlic.

He could see that the world
continued in its ignorant mirage,
its traffic and horns—limousines
disguising death

as something wrong
instead of different, the world
with its games and time,
holidays and baths.

He circled the similar towns, somnambulant
spirit unable to speak or to alter any outcome,
in sympathy with martyrs, the folly
of war, the dwindling forests . . .

Only his various isolation pursued him:
a carcass in a butcher shop,
pink streetlights after hours,
a spatter of water rounding a corner, then gone.

The weather of death was not a place,
not even a planet—yet the world kept on
turning its collar, rubbing its
damp hands as if ruin were certain—

There was no death after his death,
just a vibration, unfamiliar—still
his voice would not go back; he could not
reappear to tell them he felt the old

Sunday desires, that he was unprepared
to cross—Nor could he tarry forever entangled
with matter in earth's circumscription
where ruin was futile, finality, nowhere.

xi. Life Review

Buoyant—in the cusp of a cone, funneled by magnetic force,
it was as if he rode a raft above—something other than air,
(ether, he supposed) and when he was poised at the reach of a gyre,
and lowered onto a platform, he saw a small assembly

in robes of sculpted white-on-white brocade. Above, the glow
of receptive faces, one figure in stunning silence, gestured
toward a director's chair. The others too took places
as the room defined its borders with a screen.

He was unsure, how much time had elapsed, when
he had eaten last, if he was dreaming—was the hour
late or lean? Then the candelabras dimmed, chandeliers
recessed into the ceiling and a film began with his name in lights.

xii. Forty-Seven Years

As he watched his brief life leaf by
like a scrapbook's turning pages—he felt something
settle within the space that he'd displaced: *warmth*
from his immigrant parents, *love* from his brothers,

cousins, wife; he physically felt how he'd been their rising star,
the only one to sail through college—their pride
in his publications, his poetry and paintings. Then he saw
himself drafted west in the years of the second world war—

an army doctor attentive to burns, experiments
with the bomb. Now the affluence of the fifties—
Chief of Surgery, and at the sudden death of the father
he'd always longed to impress, he felt the growing yen

to return to New York. Jump cut to the fifty-three Caddy,
all five of them singing *Young at Heart* the speedometer close-up,
needle tapping 100 miles per hour. Expanse of desert
fading from focus, prairies, plains. Ohio. Pennsylvania—

the Holland Tunnel, at last—a new home
on Long Island's northern shore, and just as he wondered
about his fall—the scenes of his migraines began.

xiii. Migraine

What brought on the the spumy aura in the air,
      the almost euphoric spell which preceded
            primitive armies above his eyes spearing the skin?

Nauseous, fumbling for keys in a dark garage,
      he dropped his ebullient persona
            and ran for a bathroom stall.

The film rewound, then chugged fast-forward in an assault,
      camera zooming through hallways
            distorting his children's faces, silence

ovaling their mouths, his wife drawing the shades,
      the weight of a ten-ton towel over his eyebrows—Shots
            of shelves, montage of bottles spilling pills,

pharmacy samples to tranquilize and wide-angled labels smeared
      with promises to sedate. Slow-mo pan of his addictions,
            the monstrous man he'd impersonate—doors

slamming, locking, when his wife flushed the contents of a vial.
      Something blackened the space that was his body
            when each of his children froze in still-life,

blinking, turning away—his wife's strength,
      a swaying building in an earthquake.
            At last the screen dimmed into darkness

as cries ricocheted in his head,
      the family's feelings reverberating his own
            in this low-lit room

of ethereal strangers
      who sustained him
           with silver rays

of empathy and solace.

xiv. Instantly through Thought

His sorrow was heavier than his guilt
but each hung like a small dark
garment in a closet—
so this was hell.

However passive, however
accidental—his soul knew
even at the threshold of amnesia,
he'd accomplished his death

by his own hand.
And when he felt himself
occluded, a rancid star, pulled root,
too lucid in the aftermath,

the sound and shape of his thinking
warped and wafted like blown sand
until he forced his mind to create
a cage of safety,

one sacred cell, free
from self-hatred. *Yes,*
there were guides to aid him
but because he felt unworthy,

they took on the grotesque form
of lepers, roaches, rats—
Perhaps the question was
whose judgment he awaited

in this prison he'd custom-
designed, building his own
bars one at a time
instantly through thought.

xv. Self-fulfilling Prophet

It was not that he questioned his own
dead carcass but some nights he
found himself choking from thirst

in a bushy circular pit he remembered
from Dante. Here other homeless junkies
tore at their clothes in delirium tremens

or paced back and forth on leprous stumps—
At times like this he felt alive—horrifically alive.
Other nights he buzzed with slaphappy crews

of good 'ole boys, until their skin would boil
with sores he'd seen as an intern only in photos.
Then he'd leap to the street,

begging strangers for tongs and gauze,
flagging down drivers and cabs which never stopped.
Only vacuous eyes met his shouts, skittish

with ticks or practially comatose—He'd search
for shelter in boarded-up buildings
where demons crawled over

barbed wire thorns,
garbage and vermin lining the walls.
Then he'd slide down the stains of a door,

pull his knees to his throat like he did as a kid
of five or six—stripped of his
tear ducts, unable to cry,

the guilt of his shame
feeding his crime, his
unforgiving fix.

xvi. Faith Must Be a Fortress

But when the diamond of his eye
revealed conscience as counterfeit,
he saw that he was *not* his thoughts.

Without the body's encumbrance,
he saw that the mind was flawed.
a deformed crystal, thinking itself

severed from others, torn from whatever
might be God. By some imagined sin,
the mind thought of itself as *seperate,*

And if he believed that he was lost,
indeed he was—streets grew Kafkaesque
with hedges, shadows, sinister

thugs. But where was a roadside
phone booth, hospital, tow-truck?
His dread seduced him through a vortex

producing what he feared. Yet when he
dared reverse his thoughts, *Paradise*
was a bridge across the maw of his inferno,

and faith—an acropolis of roses and blue
ions sent him warm, communing rays.
Confused, his disembodied mind

doubted while vegetation withered
to streets wet with filth, hooded youths
skulking the gutters of a dicey

neighborhood. And he recognized
for the first time that he was *damned*—
Not by the mafia he thought was God
but by his own brutal judgment.

xvii. Third-eye Views

Alone, he closed his non-corporeal eyes
in the night wind and saw the face of a sphinx.
Nothing more. Not a landing to stand on.
Not an entrance to choose, nor a door to imagine
behind. The eye of the sphinx

was the mind he saw through. Was it truly *other*
or merely another sporadic reflexive
of his own sorry mystery?

Face of a sphinx. Pyramid eye of a dollar bill,
luminous through the darkness, wavering slightly
as wind, giving history a lifetime survived
by the stare of Horus, what sands leave,
Ozymandias for aeons to find . . .

He felt the eyes behind his mind
meld and dally on the runway of his brow.
At least there was somewhere to reach for,
something to soar with, leveling view,
both telescopic and holographic,

this capacious eye, a transparent mirror
somehow—above this unfocused
abyss, unblinking, but wet—

maybe a hint, maybe
something to lift
the veil.

xviii. The Wedding of Self to Selves

An open arena played on the monitor of his vision,
glossy and beveled chinks of sun, aeolian
instruments in the backdrop. Despite his penchant

for dark, he conceptualized different wishes
within the montage, and through this new eye
he perused an opera in ripples like waves from a coin

tossed into a well. Left defenseless by beautiful music,
he admitted the voices of patrons who merged
as lost parts of himself. The more he accepted, the more

he ascended from his cot where he saw his ensoulment
pooling above a bedding of self-contempt. Then voices
explained they comprised his dimensional unit,

the higher octave of each earthly history, his future, his past.
If in his recent life, he negated his worth, here beyond death
he'd return to the essence he'd always been.

Through the crack beneath his door, crepuscular streaks
leaked like a shoreline where breakers plumed over sand.
He rejoiced in a scene of his childhood beach,

Coney Island, and over the boardwalk,
he painted the weather his favorite palette
while the voices disclosed that he had full control:

No one but you creates your view. Though hidden
and buried, Spirit was carried, released
in a marriage of self to selves.

ixx. To Forget You Forgot

Grapes fermenting in heat. Grace
transfiguring each little scarab. Fixation of light
into matter. How sensibly he could imagine
Spirit's evolution now. From the mountains,
clouds skimmed the capstone, unveiling
the many mansions. The alchemist's challenge:
descent and compression. Embodied in this "vehicle"
he'd studied in med school—he realized the gnosis

of healing was just *to remember and return.*
He understood at last the mind's concretion of body,
how utterly man made his world from his Word.
Beliefs—fears, or curses, anything held and pondered
with passion, eventually hardens into form.
His intuitive spark had always examined
the body for its enigma, something perpetual,
yet abstract—but how did you locate *that?*

Cut through the heart or the grill of the brain?
To swim the film of the flesh was to journey away
from repose, caught in the warring opposites, contusions,
lymphomas, gall bladder stones—to *fall*
from transcendence, then land in that alien craft,
that closed, paradoxical shell, misplacing
your source like an Alzheimer address—
To forget you forgot—to create out of fear . . .

Husking the cob of the mind's illusions
this was the worthy surgeon's task. And he carved
his first window into a wall of his bunker, built
from a thought just beyond it—a vineyard of lapis
and tourmaline grapes, each silvered vine,
a nirvana of light—same light he'd sought
when he'd carved and cut
those essentially bestial bodies.

xx. What If Man Made the World?

Blessed with the impossible thought of green stars,
he stood by his bed and tested his power, laughing
as spontaneous stars fell like emeralds and burned

through star-shaped holes in the roof.
Was this the unfinished evolution, the Creator's
one intervention: *Remember the God in each of you?*

What if the dark thoughts walled the cities,
corrupting children, enscripting armies, shot neighbors
and strangers, cried *victim,* pointing a finger, pinning

the world on God? At once he saw through the lie
of the third dimension, saw its *reality* was off.
Sculpting his stars into one, he willed it red, reshaped it,

cutting a square at the top, boxing its ears to an orb,
throwing the whole thing out the window
as a radiant exclamation!

What if fear made the human world as it was?
Wouldn't it follow—
only fearless love could change it?

xxi. White Stone

In one instant using only his will, he created
a hill to hike, because The Ones-With-No-Names
explained the light body needs exercise

and he wanted to stretch, to make a sky
of blue-hued sparkle, climb a pile
of earth-toned rock which reminded him

of the west he had loved and been part of.
Those long drives into nothing but faded cactus
and craggy hills that hung and tumbled

over the low dust-span of road. Out of habit,
he searched for rattlers, pulling his boot up
and then he spied it—a glowing stone,

white as the light which shone through each being
made of matter, smooth and oval and speaking
a language he might have invented—

He closed his translucent fingers
and heard the rush of his name
like the whisper in which flowers grow.

Bowing his head in self-forgiveness
for his plight which had lifted and flown,
he toasted his canteen to *The All That Is*—

And in that fully-lit moment, he knew
the true second coming as grace
which would weave its gloss

beyond time around every soul.
Each unique
with its white stone.

IV

The Evening News

Thirteen Ways of Looking at Hitchcock's Blackbirds

—After Wallace Stevens & Alfred Hitchcock

I
Among the summery hems of Bodega Bay
the only moving thing
was the overseeing eye of an overweight blackbird.

II
He was of a dark Hitchcockian mind,
Like the jungle gym's tangled bars at the playground
Weighted with blackbirds.

III
The blackbirds cawed in the stillness
Anticipating their raucous role in the pantomime.

IV
A heavy-set man and a platinum blonde
Are one. A double-chinned man
And an underpaid blonde and a blackbird
Are one.

V
He did not know which to prefer,
The inflections of the cast
Or the innuendoes of the press,
The trained blackbirds' shrieking
Or the puppets rubber-banded
To the actors' wrists. The terror
Of the attic scene or her terror
Of him just after.

VI

Avian attacks filled the open fireplace
With barbaric beaks, an animated swarm.
Horror traced through the shadow
An apocalyptic cause.

VII

O swarthy fishermen of Bodega Bay,
Why do you dream of golden gulls?
Do you not see the nets around your boat shoes
Flooded with blackbirds?

VIII

I know the infatuation of the eccentric director
And his lucid, stalking rhythms.
And I know too that an ignoble obsession is involved
In what I know.

IX

When Tippi drove her silver Aston Martin
Off the set, it burnt black rubber in the path
Of one of many circular driveways.

X

At the sight of mechanical blackbirds
Striking fallen children
Even the bawds of Metro Goldwyn Mayer
Could not cry out so sharply.

XI
He rode south of San Francisco
In a glass coach.
Once, a leer pierced his eye,
In that he mistook his leading lady
For a chirping blackbird.

XII
The film's frames are still playing.
Royalty registers must still be chiming.

XIII
It was 1963 all afternoon.
Rooks and plovers were screeching
And they were going to screech.
In her torn green suit,
Tippi hid in the cedar limbs.

Corona Spring

—after Mariangela Gaultieri

We did not make the sky. No. Nor the birds
that entrain and lift together in large numbers
through collective, intuitive moves. And we

did not make the moon, or the grass, or
the sand that falls through the hourglass as if
in our finitude we understood all the blessings

of time. So when it stopped, tied us
to our tracks, left us to flail and rail
on the hem of our thoughts,

something was wrought, something
new . . . to show us we make things
together. We do. We make the weather,

make children and dinner to share.
We offer the rice and the wine. It's not
that we have no power. Aren't we made

in the shape of our maker? We
stopped to discover new orders
keeping our distance from one another—

We enter our hearts, falling together,
pulling apart, tumbling out of our masks,
out of our minds that try to analyze,

to rationalize, blind as a bat
bumping its black fuzzy body
into the rafters of blame—

ratchetting down from the roof of the attic
where ancestral histories are stored.
We must play in this global game,

must unmask the dust and the dark,
must dig down to dig up,
look for—and hold up the sky,

believing we also make light.

Rewind

The walls of the two towers pick up their plaster and dust draws upwards into blue. Those who jumped—don't—but blow softly up through open windows to sit at their desks intact. Two hundred firemen moonwalk back to their trucks, hang hoses up like warriors' swords as the running pedestrians stop, spin on their heels and stroll back through park and plaza shops. The melted church rights its ribs, pulls the roof back on like a hat, while fallen spires resurrect from blueprints. Both aircraft tanks siphon back flames of gas. Glass mosaic uncoils from debris, folds into steel archways. Two planes resume their flight to Los Angeles . . . and Los Angeles . . . as white exhaust feathers through morning, early and clear. Three thousand busy people loved by others, still right here. Gorgeous, that Indian-summer sky.

Perish The Thought

Perishing to the right of us, perishing to the left, as we walk
among the six billion. And there, but for the grace of the gods,
we go. Our pets chomp the dust, our jazziest cars, our glamour-
girl actresses, all the Hollywood studs. We've been hanged
and beheaded, poisoned and stoned, disemboweled and tied
to the stake—At the mercy of dictators, soldiers, spouses and
popes. The Cemetery of Perishables runs miles and miles,
overseen by stone angels whose chipped fingers coil like snakes.
The Sphinx even ages, she passes slowly, watching the rest of us
lepers from eon to eon rapidly rot No one is *not* perishing. No
republic, no empire, no island nation. Even Rome was shredded
by Saxons and Goths. The pagan gods are breathless now.
As mortal as rock stars. Only they're real stars, burnt out
and ashen, thumb-tacked onto the night.

What Words?

What Words could fold this paper back into a tree?
How can I coax its ridges back into bark, rub its creases
into nodules, flatten its already concave belly
for someone to carve a note to the green world

that we have not intended such forest-sorrow?
That we're merely lax, hungry people, unhappy
and often lazy—How could we have better read the signs
from the nesting tree-hearts when we made motors,

sheared limbs, lit fires, and laid one board over another
dividing space from space to hold more *things?*
We're worried now there's no way back to the words
our ancestors sing. All the rivers are damned

and directed. Do the bridges know global positions?
Does soil beneath buildings feel each aching acre
where once was an orchard? Hard to imagine
whose idea it was to hide missiles in silos among pastures

and meadows in God's backyard. Will our exhaust
banish the stars until we have nothing to read by
but our own glaring florescence? We recall chewing roots
as in an old dream, how they offered themselves,

promised the knowledge to temper all we've mastered
blindly. Even the Tree of Life's violation comes down
to a vellum invitation. Hospitals offer oxygen ridden
with airborne diseases. There's no air in the air there—

Tell me what spell to conjure, my dear disposables
to free you from input and output, stacking
and shredding. What can I say to get you to share
your healing shelter, your flowering secrets,
birded branches to hold us in shade once again?

Toxic Soup

Some say civilizations begin inside stars.
Or at the periphery of a black hole.
If that's the case, as ours will end,
another may be born. Our blood gone

kryptonite, we're glowing from within
as short waves fade in the ionosphere,
coronas flare and limbs of solar disks
flip tunes to acid rain. And while

our high-def amps the living room's
blue ambience with barium, our
inner circuitry gets played. We stand
like zombies in fluoridated showers,

consume flesh that fed on poisoned corn
our F.D.A. approves, and we don't see
the vast light-belt of photon cloud,
how it pours down its love.

Rock on Magnetic Redirect—
where poles rotate and realign—
Let interstitial romance frack and frack,
while rattled platelets of the planet,

uptick to earth and quake—and quake
as overwrought emotions circumambulate
the globe in rings of sulphorific breath.
Bodies converge with chemtrails, cellular

frequencies, Corona's toxic thoughts.
Earthlings, your core is hazardous—
Wake up Wake up Wake up Wake up!

The Evening News

It's another option if you're ruling out suicide.
Ruin rents the land and vermillion limns the fires.
Wires scorch down the spines of weight-bearing walls.
Rain rusts dull as a dismal stone in gravel.

We could pull names from a cave, lob Molotov cocktails,
hug all the bastards killing each other. As prayers
huddle in the heart's bunker, let's surf to the preachers,
priests and mullahs, wild with brimstone and belief—

Can't they see we're *all* The Second Coming?
Watch the sea spiral forth inside the earth's church,
feel the vectoring in her breakers—Look—
heaven's right here, absolute, utero blue.

Color Blind

It's just a glitch in the filament field, a recessive
gene found mostly in men whose gray shades extend
beyond fifty—And thank God they can read

the position of stoplights and know when to stop, when
to go—while their light inside is a flash of cinquefoil
that spins up the spinal chakras so they're open

to shades of raiment. The one with the massive absence
of violet in his veins still feels the passion of purple,
and the one missing green is still nourished—

though by a world dressed in tungsten—
and what must they see in the torque
of blue ocean? Dun-colored breakers?

Celluloid nitrate and camphor? The Spring sky
in Vermont? *But wait*—Think shadow and mystery,
film noir shot through the bay to a lantern-lit room,

shot through slats of venetian blinds, silhouette
of a heat-packing moll on the wall, the smoke
of her hips as she presses herself into hiding,

blur of ash in the air—oh, the wash of that whisper—
rain on the gravel outside—and rain on the felt
brim of the hat pulled low for the exit . . .

Few things in this life are black and white. But imagine—
you knew how to step through the nooses of darkness,
how to slip out the sleeve of your duster, shed the finalé

of color right down to your luminous skin.

The Harmony of the Next

When concerned with the first factor, are you too blind
to see the harmony of the next? Suppose the charge
and damage occurred so prematurely you can't move over
the rough knuckle of your habitual relapse? The way your teeth
worry the skin and you're in the dark and out of band aids
and don't notice night turning to dawn on the flip side
of the planet. That confusion, that morning drama whose station
you never switch. What if the first factor is only a figment,
The Phantom of Threshold Crossings, nano-moments
after your sun rocks into the sea? Imagine the children
in China smiling as light gluts the kitchens where
mothers heat milk, and school bells ring out over the nutmeg,
over the violet villages under lavender mountains.

Beauty

Death is The Mother of . . .
　　—Wallace Stevens

Beauty was the name of Barbara's cat who got torn apart by a dog, and Beauty's the name of the young girl who released a prince from his curse of fur by learning to love a beast. Beauty wins daily over brains in Hollywood and on T.V. though some would say it doesn't last unless you're a cube of sky, the peak of a mountain or a tropical wave and even they must contend with shadows and clouds, especially when seen through the eyes of someone whose beautiful life's about to change—

Even *dark* can be beauty, *dark* as in tragic, when what is rendered from loss exposes a wound that means something whole and perfect prevailed for at least a moment and then it's a shimmering absence in space where once was an essence so mystical you could almost hear it pray. And you miss its deep sighing, the way Barbara misses her cat, *a beautiful missingness,* the way I miss the beast who left me with longing—

since beauty is always fleeting. We think we love for other reasons— Beauty alone doesn't earn true love (and there's a little beauty in *that.)* But even death transmutes to beauty, casting a coil, relic, shell, the concave stone that fits your thumb, sunlight fading its palette the hue of water pumped up from wells. We can mourn the loss of beauty, its warm pastels,
its moaning knell.

The All Which is All

Beneath the feet of arithmetic lie the nine integers
upon which the body of all measurements stands.
The All which is All. And I have waited a lifetime
to meet it. That gentle containment like the chalice

of morning when the sun is just ten thousand
centimeters behind the fog. That gravitational pull
into balance—And now I'm waltzing from room to room
wearing the music of one seismic tone, reaching

for my prayer book—Glory be to the numerals
holding the chords of our firmament intact.
Light spectrum drumming, picture window
beating time with the linen roses on the sofa,

so I recline between Latin syllables, between
vowels of psalms and the sighs of Isaiah—
while you boil water for coffee, the oven of loving
set to some safe estimation of Fahrenheit.

Aquarian Orpheus

Remembering Mark Strand, 1934-2014

It's as if he knows how close he's always been to Spirit.
As if your hand might pass through the numen of his voice
and a little shadow shiver on the auditorium wall. If you asked,
I bet he'd glance away with a half-smile and husky whisper . . .
Everything ages . . . We get old . . . Everyone disappears . . .

And this with a hissing sigh: . . . *Love fades* . . . But his eyes
would twinkle like wild dice and you'd know underneath
that haunting still lives a romantic, why else would he strike us
so humble, so droll? One could do worse than scribble ethereal
while years slip by as pages lifted by wind. Maybe he sees

something we can't imagine beyond our timeline. Always his
quavery moans purr like a couple of mongrels, wounded but
playful. *Oh Strand! Oh Handsome Strand!* Your towering gaze
taught us tricks that held out mystery, ships made from words,
lifelines we almost grasp as we hear poems built of vowels, poems

mocking themselves, poems so pleased to be poems, bemused
at the range of their pain, consumed with their own toiling
well into twilight—elusive, mewing poems whose feet never touch
ground. And here in the pin-drop quiet, ten deep
in the standing-room-only of his vapory breath, we're almost

splay-legged in rapture while there at the podium, he's merely
mouthing the syllables of light and air and glass in the perfectly
stitched font of *The New Yorker.* We could sail the rictus
of his cryptic grin, its crescent aisle, while we cling to his piper's
cape and flow from the building down an embankment where wind

blows color out of the gloaming and the smoky poems dissolve,
deliquescent as rain, beclouding the synchronous rise of birds. And
Strand, with the bittersweet smile, glad to have touched our lives,
never giving a hoot who mimicked him, he just keeps moving,
holy over the fields, an Acuarian Orpheus, one with his head intact,

toes dangling over the edge of our good green planet
into the mythic skies, taking his place beside Homer, Virgil,
Demosthenes' stones under his tongue, back to the first
bicameral tribe, the blue mother cave where he first dreamed
in silence the tender language of the newly born.

"Sounds Bouncing From Stones"

—a line from Forest Gander

Stones know the sheaves of earth's hidden scrolls.
Stones sculpt themselves for millennia,

strong hearts beneath smooth skins, pulsing, alive—
though they're made into tombs, into walls. Nights

when stars are near and the moon casts its milk
for sky creatures to suckle, stones call to each other

with heat absorbed from the sun. They glow and go golden.
Sound sings through my brain while walking alone, sings

in a language I think I don't know. But the thoughts I receive
in those moments are sky-blown and holy. I bow to the moon,

which is also a stone and The Scroll of the World Soul
opens—cuneiform-full, like glyphs in a cave

hung with crystal-eyed bats. What is true in the daylight
no longer holds. Sounds spill through the quarries'

harmonics, a clandestine chorus and stone tunes
throb through me like steam. Stonebeat. Batbeat.

Omphalos. I'm remembering home from forever ago.

V

Without and Within

Sun Song

I thank the sun that charges sand, charges landscape, fuses clouds,
defuses densities and colors—Sunrise—the beginning of rhythm,
that ballet of lift-to-rise within the sky's furnace, like the history
of music, percussive shimmy and pulse announcing the global
light codes—Wasn't it sun that birthed creation? Spark at its center
waah-waah-ing into *BANG*—Vertical strings begetting earth's
heating and cooling, begetting spirals spinning her platelets,
begetting illusions of time… Ancient Egyptians swarmed
on their knees to greet atoms stirring open each day. Thrice

Great Hermes, his arcane alchemy—a young boy's urine,
the Pelican's capacious jaw, promises spawned from maracas
of morning caws, droning didgeridoos, deep respirations
of light that drum to synchronize our D.N.A. so we perceive
collectively in awe. Earth preceded our human presence. . .
such mystery before the "known"—until one day,
subjective awareness triggered the egos' woes. Caesars
fancied themselves the sun's descendants before Vikings
and Goths called it an arrogant masculine star. And to the soft-
sided, in-sighted, (think *female,* think priestess, or goddess),

sweet blossoms of wisdom in oxytocin! If the sun were mine,
I wouldn't freeze it in photographs but keep it coming,
*be*coming—a model Messiah—a husband with whom to slip
into caves where candles ignite and cobwebs are swept
to make room for merciful warmth. Call me Darwinian-
heliotropic: *I feel therefore I turn toward light!*
Let shine sing acapella in the susurrus of ocean while
I swallow my Gregorian dawn. Let rhythmic stars trail off
as light migrates through flesh with threads of fire,
through diamond-faceted dust—The sun, *the sun* is song.

Noah's Dove

Ark at the bottom of the deep globe, listing
in unsteady waves. Nothing out the port holes.
He'd almost given up. Rain, so long, so much,
the ship itself shrunk to a bottle of underworld

blue. Animals uncoupling, uneasy in salty dreams,
some coiled seasick against walls, some
just come from sleep, yearning for mesas
jungles, plains. The cubits Noah calibrated

were mere cubicles. Giraffes and camels had no view.
Rats gnawed the oars. No one yipped, barked, hissed,
ribbited, growled or meowed. The sleeping wheezed
and palmed the air. Some sensed the end

of earth though no one told them so.
The last day Noah swept his eyes of fog
and panned the pewter sky to bring her home.
Branch in beak, she flew—Like Venus

wearing moonstone, midwife
in service, *Beneditctas viriditas*
between ratcheting wings.

Without and Within

They could no longer return to whence they came
but neither could they leave the place they entered. Christ came.
Those who had come, he brought out;
and those who had gone out, he brought in.

—*The Gospel of Philip, The Nag Hammadi Library*

Such comings and goings! In and out, body and spirit,
the disincarnate looking for home and not finding it

in the body alone. Looking for home, but alone
in the body and therefore—descendent. Believing

the self alone when home was near. We only need
to be in gnosis and know the hidden from within,

from where it is sown. Spirit, unmanifest, is breath
and by breath is manifested, ascendant. To be cognizant,

to know Sprit is without is always known by kin,
known by all who exist in gnosis—as all *are* kin;

even those without are kin in their oneness within.
Without question. *All.* Without and within.

Qumran

*Mary of Bethany asked him, "Will the thirst for knowledge
ever be quenched?"*
                    —The Gnostic Gospel of Thomas

In the scriptorium ruin, I set foot in a life I knew
as a recluse draped in a bone-white robe, sequestered
from the city's first century sects. I remembered
we hadn't fled to stone caves, we withdrew—
like a wave pulls from sand. And we entered an ocean

of desert, not far from the Dead Sea where everything
floats and even the salt breathes—so remote—
the only sounds were the quills scratching on parchment,
recording Yeshua's alternate journey, the one with Magdalene
as companion. We were so certain—the Kingdom

was on its way, that each new day in our cursed world
might be the last. That apocryphal light was rising
behind the beveling sky's glass, where the future lapped
at the edges of clouds. As I fingered stones in my pockets,
I sensed the earth's hertz and walked up limestone steps

leading to nothing but the remains of one wall.
Under the spell of a scorching sun, an archway opened
to a corridor with columns, where the ghosts of Essenes,
busy with bread and olives, busy with cisterns and clay cups—
floated as if they could pull me with their touch

through the frequency of twenty centuries passing.
I closed my eyes and swayed my body
in time with what I'd forgotten
as it held me in lustration so hot it mated
with darkness, then transmuted, the way black

contains the whole spectrum of color. I stilled myself there,
starlings squawked overhead and when I heard
Romans horses stop dead, I rushed into the present,
came to myself blinking—as the sky drew closer.
And I knew in the way of gnosis—watched

the translucent past swim into the sea—
Basking my face in the glow of what had dissolved,
I was suddenly called with the other tourists
to board the bus back to Jerusalem.

Presence

To wake without the hands of tomorrow's clock,
without the words of yesterday's narration, the whole heft

of personal detail, quotidian tasks—*Poof*—
flecks of water where night was. Then growth

like the hibiscus's infinite petals, stamens
and stems. Those fragrant extended seconds

of presence. Oh, to be the conscious creator
of each linear segment . . . *Yes!* Then do the minutia

without worry, as Zen says—When you sweep,
Sweep! Oh, the mercy, the alchemy

of not thinking . . . All one undoing of everything
in the mind. So to do without is more, is most.

Rocking

Not quite a tomboy, eyes scowling behind shaggy bangs, two
skinny braids—I was a girl who liked needles of sun on the back
of my legs. Jump rope and hop scotch with my sister or the girls
next door, baseball with my brothers, the birch tree for first,
shrubs for second, the left leg of the swing set for third
and the pink Spalding ball could clear the privet hedge
when I slugged it. After a hard day's play, I loved the way
dusk came as if on a dimmer, blue bulb slowly lowered
till the sky released that sapphire-crayon shade. I'd push
the kitchen screen, plop down by the window, heels hooked

on the chair's bottom rung—and there, I would rock.
Arms crossed, rock back and forth to my own stroke
of systole and diastole, my meditation with no mantra,
though I'd find some melodic counterpart on the horizon,
maybe the breath of the earth's great core—Nestled inside,
 I felt safe. Soothed by my own hypnosis. I made no noise,
yet always a hungry sibling came by to check on dinner
and told me to stop. My mother accused me of her headache,
my sister said I bothered the dog and my nervous
grandmother regarded my habit as institutionally insane.

But I'd turn them all off, rocking and rocking, touched by
some precognition of return, womblike or tomblike—
I can't be sure, maybe the dance of a whirling Sufi,
or the dizzying priestess of some pagan god—this metronomic
buzz left me *alive* in the throb of all my antennae. This
was an other-dimensional place, a wave inside a drum,
hum inside a cave, a solace I rarely recover—
have never recovered from.

What Touches

Too many pillows on the bed of your body.
What are they hiding there above the sateen sheets?
Displacement that holds your imprint?

The soul's enchantment into form?
Do your arms fit the sleeves of dreams
dreamt in the fit of elixirs fixed on the nightstand?
And where is the door to the temple, the body

as diamond, as ingress into dimension? Or the body
as sacred housing, as golden dome? As blanket, hiding
what is meant to bide secret under the soul's skin,

too tarnished to reveal itself fully? There's folly
in disbelieving the leaving, believing only
the left form. Not the conceivable leaving

as entrance to elsewhere. What touches
then lets drop. Not the step through the mandorla,
but the inexorable going back.

Your Name

Someone, something—whispers your name.
Or it's only the fan there on your desk and
the noise of moving air that propels it
across the ceiling, skimming an open window,
it's your name in invisible ink splayed on the walls.
Why then do you think it's an echo or ghost
saying something important when it's only
your name, the patient syllables blown
through the room, the shimmying space,
as if your name had a hand you could hold,
as if a phantom lover stood in the ozone
beside the bed, or an angel with huge burning
wings, long locks, strands of gold singeing
his shoulders, when it's only the fan
that responds to your yanking the cord,
blades winged into silence . . . falling dead
in the air, filling the room with the contours
of quiet, the round pronouncement of vowels,
wilted letters like underwear tossed on the chair.

Limbo

You prepare
to float one foot in front
of the other, to move

because you're stuck.
A low ceiling overhead, a few
stalactites poke

motivation. Underfoot,
earth. That which could serve
as telluric vibration.

To the left, a wall. To the right,
another. Locked up. Locked in. Held
by sands in the hourglass

and the shroud that covers the body,
linen over the skin
that shelters the bones,

the marrow deep down
and within—a living heart
on repeat, its lone note.

I've heard it
called "tomb time."
Even Christ

needed three days
between crucifixion
and resurrection.

Something Other

When, in the hours prior to dawn, you apprehend
the sentient existence of others like insistent insects

in the room—buzzing, hovering, hover and buzz
and you believe they must belong to you, frames of the past

that is still here or the future that never comes but is present
like the formulas for perfect storms are present always, always

incipient fledglings because the potential somethingness
of space and form doesn't stop, and everything, each river, each

evolving rock, each cloud careening on the wind's rails
keeps transforming into something else, something other—

so when you hear them, it is with an ear inside your mind,
your ears inside their ears perhaps, though it is your hands

that fly to your forehead batting away the buzz above the fan's
breath, between its electrons, beneath the outside stars that arrive

in the cave of your head and light up the moon's language, whose
words though foreign possess a familiar sense of song—sometimes

aria, sometimes dirge—is it a truth you knew in utero, that moving
stillness? And you wonder when your spirit finally bridges

the etheric and leaves this grave living to enter their adjacent
dance, where will you arrive then? And will you ever think

of them as *fact,* the way we are led to think spinning atoms
make matter? When your presence is past, your absence,

already inchoate, will you recognize your own becoming?

Eve of My Evolution

I'm off to the church bazaar in my mind
that implodes on Saturday nights
when I talk down the moon from its monthly
dementia. I watch the stars out city windows
as reckless as I am—inconstant astronomy
ringing like old switchboard phones.
Each night I revisit the ozone of girlhood
and wake up in thunder. I wasn't yet three
the first time I heard an invisible voice.
Waking my mother, nudging into her bed,
I asked what she wanted—After that
I heard the insides of songs as blue mysteries.
The higher I pumped on the swing set,
the deeper into my throat they'd drown.
Something spoke in the blades of fans
and under the hood of my Dad's new car.
Like sky creeps into the throat of a bird
to keep it aloft—I'm pregnant with
what language lost when it took on sound.

Here for the Thanking

Sometimes it's all you can do to bear the brilliant moment.
Then you remember—here is the earth. Look around,
here is the crazy planet, all rainbowed abalone,

all carnival glass, the whorl of colors about to shatter . . .
But your feet stick, and even upside down,
the sky is a blanket, a gentle embrace whether blue

or gray, and the moon too, even when faded in daylight
as you trudge through godawful traffic, even when sun
has dried like an overcooked egg in a skillet, edges

luffing—here is light that comes without bidding,
that offers itself buck-naked to keep you from spinning
out into the nowheres, down black holes

into underground mold. It's then you inhabit
appreciation for basic living and *joy*—Here are my feet
in their soiled sneakers still stuck to the sand,

not swept away into alien tides and here is my breath
surging through the appendages of my body,
here my third eye within, reading all shades

of the ocean. No need to imagine beyond,
here for the taking, here for the worship,
and for the thanking now and anon—.

Intelligent Design

The impulse towards union was already there in our protoplasm.
Love in our genes.
Irreversible love.
                                    —Ernesto Cardenal

This late in human history, can you imagine the species
            as newly sculpted clay, rewired without the will-to-evil?
                        Could war cries dilate into chimes or chords

and chants, so that the longing on the planet would morph
            into *be*-longing? A planet of mutual accord?
                        Given the chance, our different drummers pealing

with chimes, would we dilate the pumps of the four-chambered
            heart? Imagine frequencies which stun the stars
                        zithering our veins, old pains chimed up

and chanted out—molded anew into that utopian nonsense
            we studied in high school, no longer
                        nonsense now, a species beyond Darwinian

damnation—*Imagine* new chords in the higher octaves
            of the skies, music so rich with chiming, nights whose
                        moons transmute the coast of a species

newly minted, newly accorded a space beyond ancient science,
            beyond the sinister remnants of religions' divisions.
                        The past—important not to forget, but more

important to surpass—Imagine chimes climbing the spinal cords
            through the body's orchestra, all that irradiating power,
                        nothing but irreversible love

            issuing from our meager world.

122

What Falls Away is Elsewhere

—after Roethke, Stevens, Yeats

In the changing climate of my heart, I live by the sea's genius,
its sunken coral dream seals the sand in breakers

at the edge of my painted toes. I love to swim
and take my swimming slow. My body, holy body,

feels by thinking where to go, it rides the clouds
acquainted with the glassy sun. Light takes

my eyes and wakes and washes them among emblazoned
white caps, fiery zones. Fish and fowl fly and peck,

seek and scavenge, and know not what we are
or what is passing or to come—But I take the morning

stroking skies acutest at their singing, swim where
I can shimmy through some fragrant portal

into all my being's dance, dying into hues of gold,
and deeper still, through summer sounds—the sea

is not a mask—what else is there to know?
What's misbegotten dies, what falls away is elsewhere,

always dimly-starred on high horizons. Nature
has so many things to do, gong-tormented like ourselves,

and soul-clapped—like our origins.

Notes

* There are references to alchemy in the poems "the Tree at Tigertail," "Presence" and "Sun Song." In the first poem, the alchemical transformation of lead into gold or the symbolic transmutation of the soul, also the words "emerald" and "cobalt" refer to the alchemical texts. *The Emerald Tablet,* is one of the most famous, attributed to Hermes Trismegistus, a combination of Hermes, the Hellenic god, (aka Mercury, the catalytic substance of the alchemical process) and the Egyptian god known as Thoth. Cobalt blue is used in glass alchemy. The references to the Pelican and the "young boy's urine" indicate symbolic stages of the process, part of the procedure to create the "white stone" according to C.G. Jung. The Pelican was thought to pierce its own breast with its beak and feed its young with its own blood and symbolizes the Christ sacrifice and another stage in the creation of the Red Stone.

* "The Tree at Tigertail" for a dear friend, Cara Nusinov, was written during a visit at her Casa in Coconut Grove.

* "The Night as Meditation" plays on Wallace Stevens poem's title "The World as Meditation" which is also about Penelope missing Odysseus.

* In "Indulgences," and "What Touches" the "mandorla" is from the Italian, "almond," an oval shape often seen as an aureole or halo in medieval art, also as a symbolic gateway.

* "What Falls Away is Elsewhere" plays with lines from Roethke's famous Villanelle "I Wake to Sleep," Yeats' "Byzantium" and Stevens' "The Idea of Order at Key West."

*"The World's Veil" was influenced by the philosophy of *The Course in Miracles.*

* "Corona Spring" takes the line "We did not make the sky" from a poem by the Italian poet, Mariangela Gaultieri.

About the Author

Deborah DeNicola is the author of six poetry books, *Where Divinity Begins* (Alice James Books), *Original Human,* (WordTech Press), for which she received her fifth Pushcart Nomination, *Inside Light,* (Finishing Line Press), *Harmony of the Next* (2005) which won the Riverstone Chapbook Award, *Psyche Revisited* (1992), which won the Embers Magazine Chapbook Contest and *Rainmakers* (Coyote Love Press). Her spiritual memoir, and Amazon Best Seller, *The Future That Brought Her Here* from Nicholas Hays/Ibis Press, was a best seller in Psychology on Amazon.com in Sept 2009, and won an Honorable Mention at the Los Angeles Book Festival in 2013. Deborah compiled and edited the anthology *Orpheus & Company; Contemporary Poems on Greek Mythology* from The University Press of New England, and in 2008 won the Analytical Essay Award from *Packingtown Review* and The Santa Barbara Poetry Award, the first-place award from Briar Cliff Review Poetry Competition in 2006 and *Carpe Articulum's* first place in their 2010 Poetry Contest. In 2013 her short story won The Carol Bly Short Story competition. She was awarded a Poetry Fellowship in 1997 from the National Endowment for the Arts, William T. Foley Award from *America,* The Barbara Bradley Award from The New England Poetry Club, and a Special Mention from *The Pushcart Prizes 1992.* She has been a Bread Loaf Scholar, a recipient of fellowships from The MacDowell Colony, The Centrum Foundation, The Virginia Center for the Creative Arts, and The Vermont Studios. She served as Poetry reviewer for *The Ft. Lauderdale Sun Sentinel* and was a contributing editor for the *South Florida Poetry Journal,* She has been an adjunct professor at Massachusetts College of Art, Lesley University in Cambridge, MA, and Broward College in South Florida. Deborah teaches writing and dream image workshops online. Her web site is www.intuitivegateways.com.

www.ingramcontent.com/pod-product-compliance
Lightning Source LLC
Chambersburg PA
CBHW070333090426
42733CB00012B/2465